MY RAINBOW TO KEEP

MICHELLE L. JEFFREYS

CONTENTS

IN MEMORY

Zoë,

Thank you for being my light for fourteen beautiful years. Love, Mom

In memory of Zoë Raine Galasso
2/22/2000 - 10/24/2014

DEDICATION

To my son, Rayden, thank you for showing me the meaning of true love. You are the driving force behind my desire to become a better person every day.

Son, no matter our lost time, my love for you has never faltered. Thank you for coming back to me so we can continue on our healing journey together. We have been through the worst, my son, but together, I know we will emerge stronger.

I dedicate this book to you, Rayden. I could never have written it without your support and encouragement.

To my daughter, Lotte, thank you for choosing me to be your mother. You arrived at a time when I needed you most. You brought joy back into my life when I thought I would never see it again. I dedicate this book to you as well.

INTRODUCTION

For years, I had a deep desire to write my story. I tried on several occasions. Each time the process was the same. I would begin time and again only to decide against it for many reasons. I didn't know where to start, the timing was off, or the content did not flow right. The excuses piled up, I had doubt, and I grappled with how to honor my child in the best light. I wondered how the public would interpret my thoughts as they read them. I struggled with how I wanted the book to be perceived.

In the early days of my grief, a book wasn't even a consideration. However, I felt compelled to write so starting a blog seemed doable. It was more personable, and I was in complete control of who I let into my world. Plus, it just seemed more natural to me. I could write when I felt inclined to write and share when I felt the desire to do so.

Today, the blog is doing so well. It has become a tool for other parents who have lost children. It is a place where grieving parents can make sense of the many emotions they experience.

The decision to finally move forward on this book came after receiving countless emails from blog visitors recounting their appreciation for how much the blog helped them through their grief journey. Those emails gave me the courage to share my story with a broader audience. Thank you to my blog readers for the prompting and support.

This book is written to honor my child, Zoë, who was tragically, and unexpectedly, taken from me. The accounts I share shed some light on the grieving process from a first-hand account. I hope the emotions and experiences that I endured through the worst possible experience will help others through their grief.

I don't think there is anything worse than losing someone you love more than life itself. To grieve that loss alone just adds to the pain. This book is my attempt at demonstrating to others who are suffering that they are not alone. Someone out there has been through something similar. We may be able to help you get through the tough times. Please check out my website/blog at www.healingthruwellness.com.

Dear reader, this book was not easy to write. Being open and raw is hard. Vulnerability is difficult for me and re-living the toughest experience of my life to write this book was extremely taxing. However, I believe it is important to tell your story if you truly want to heal. You don't have to write a book, but I encourage you to share with someone. For me, writing was just another step in the grieving process. Sharing our stories is important because it gives hope to others in need. I spent too many years masking my pain when ultimately, I just wanted the freedom to release it. Until now, I did not give myself the permission to do so. I believe this book is a step in the right direction. I am officially declaring the freedom to share my journey of healing with you so I can courageously continue down the right path.

In my early years of grief, reading about other's losses provided justification for what I was feeling and helped me feel less alone. I learned there is no right or wrong way to grieve and that everyone's journey is different. There is no timeline for grief. What worked for some may not work for others. One thing I do know is that although grieving may never end and it can feel very isolating, it is important that we find a way to navigate through it. This book is my way of sharing the tools that have worked for me, in the hope that they may help you through your journey. Perhaps my approach can work for you.

I also wanted to show people what a tragedy looks like long-term. I experienced a high profile, tragic event. For weeks, the only thing people saw was the media reports. However, the sensationalism only lasted until the next big headline arrived. No one understood what happened after the news stopped. In my case, the pain didn't end when the world's interest in the story did. I live every day of my life trying to manage the hurt and sorrow, all while the world around me continues.

My most authentic intent in writing this book is to invite my readers to see my beautiful daughter outside of that tragic headline. I want you to know her as I knew her. She was a precious and vibrant girl with a bright future. I want people to know the person she was and could have been. To share her story, I have to tell my own. It is important for me to say her name, to honor the life she did have, and acknowledge the life she should have had. I also want to encourage those of you who are suffering by showing you that we can move forward even when we don't think it is physically possible.

During my story you may feel anger and sadness, and at other times I hope you feel joy, peace, and hope. It is not my desire for anything I share to trigger events you may have experienced. So, if you need to take a break from reading, please do so. Do not push yourself to read anything beyond what you are ready for. I want this book to be an encouragement. I welcome you into my story.

CHAPTER 1
ANY GIVEN DAY

No one wakes up in the morning thinking a tragic event is going to occur. We start the day as normal following often mundane practices on autopilot. How many times have you driven to work only to arrive wondering how you got there? Seriously, I know I am not the only one.

People usually do not prepare for a tragedy, because we do not see it coming at all. It is nowhere on the radar, and it never should be. We go about our days living our best lives as we learn, grow, and create better lives for ourselves.

This was me; I went about my days thinking only forward. How can I improve my current surroundings, improve myself, and make life better for my children? After I had my two older kids, I was fortunate to stay home with them, but as they became older, it was time for me to go back to work.

I had gained quite a bit of weight when I was pregnant so my first step to self-improvement started with the decision to get back into martial arts and join the YMCA. I quickly dropped fifty pounds and fell in love with fitness again. As a teenager, I was on the swim team, practiced martial arts, did gymnastics, and performed as a cheerleader. I was also an extrovert and felt energized around people. I naturally connected with others.

Working out and getting to know people at the local YMCA pushed me toward my career in health and wellness. I worked my way from member services to weight room attendant, and I took the required courses and certifications to become a personal trainer and Yoga instructor. I began working at other YMCA locations, wellness centers, and eventually as a contracted yoga instructor on a Navy base. What started out as a part-time position turned into a permanent, full-time position as the Fitness Manager. I had found my dream job.

The Navy provided all the necessary training that I needed to become certified in all forms of group fitness, personal training, and nutrition counseling. They also put me through two years of college for a certification in Organizational Leadership. I began to thrive in my career as well as with my peers. I loved creating an environment where sailors and their families could feel safe, gain knowledge of health and wellness, and have fun.

My job became so fulfilling, I felt like everything was in place. My children were getting older, and I was able to provide for them. Life finally seemed to be working out the way I imagined. Although thriving in my career, my personal life was suffering, and I would soon find myself in the middle of an amicable divorce.

The week of Zoë's death, I was instructing Sailors on Command Fitness during a weeklong course. In this course, we taught physically-fit Sailors how to implement a fitness program at their command. This is always a long week filled with early mornings, late evenings and a lot of paperwork.

As fun as the training weeks were, I always looked forward to the half day on Fridays at the end of the course. On this day the Sailors take their final exam, get their certifications, take a group photo and say farewell.

Friday arrived, and I was exhausted. I sat down in my boss's office to reflect and relax after a long week of coursework. I remember chatting, laughing, and telling her all about the fun filled week we had just had. We talked about where we were going for happy hour and what we had left to finish for the day. Spirits were high, and nothing could prepare us for what came next.

We heard a knock on the door....

CHAPTER 2
WHEN TRAGEDY STRIKES

On October 24th, 2014, at 10:39 am my daughter took her last breath. That is the day that is forever etched in my memory. From that day forward, my family, other victims' families, the community, and everyone's sense of security was forever changed.

Zoë went to school just like any ordinary day. She picked out her outfit, did her hair and makeup, grabbed a quick breakfast, then headed off to school. She had no idea what awaited her. A "friend" invited her to lunch, and like any other child she was probably excited to be included. But he wasn't inviting her to lunch. It was an invitation to her death. He had pre-meditated her murder. I feel devastation and anger well up as I type those evil words.

The lunch started out normal. As the kids sat at the lunch table, chatting amongst themselves, laughing, and going on with their day, Zoë's "friend" pulled a handgun out of his backpack. Before anyone could react, they were targeted and shot one by one. I don't believe they even knew what hit them. I find peace in the hope that my daughter never knew what was coming and that she just went to sleep. I used to allow my mind to imagine what her last moments could have been like. I would find myself traveling down a very dark route. I have learned restraint over the years to not allow my mind to go there. I had to realize that that path offered nothing in the way of healing. It couldn't change what happened. Instead, it only offered despair.

As I sat at work in my boss's office, a coworker entered the room and shared the horrific news unfolding about a high school shooting. At first, I thought, "Oh no, this is terrible!" and my heart went out to the victims. Then as the news became clearer, I realized it was my child's school. Unbelievably, I still did not think this would happen to me, that this would involve my children. But my worst nightmare had just become reality.

The next thing I remember is being handed my phone and seeing the numerous text messages from my ex-husband and son. There were none from Zoë. We were all in a panic at this stage. No one knew what to think, do, or say. I remember going outside, clutching the wall, and having my first panic attack. My friend Diana picked me up and held me close as we both tried to grasp what was happening.

After racing home, I spent the next few hours continuously calling and texting Zoë, but to no avail. I made sure my son was safe at a nearby church, and his dad was on his way there to get him. Rumors were flying about who the children were that were shot, but no one could confirm any of it. I received numerous texts and phone calls from friends sending me hope and praying for our family. We finally heard that the children involved were being transported to the hospital, so we went.

Once there, we were ushered into a large waiting area which was blocked off for trauma victims. As I sat there, feeling sick to my stomach, not knowing if my child was alive, I looked around at all the people in the waiting room. I saw the other victims' families and I started to realize that my child was a part of this. These were her friends' parents, and it sickened me even more. I will never forget the number of friends and family that sat with me that day. I can picture them all clearly as we sat there with heads bowed, occasionally glancing at each other, and sending unspoken hope.

After what seemed like hours, we were finally called back to a separate room to speak to some doctors. As I sat in that room, fearing the worst, I remember them coming in and asking questions about Zoë. What was she wearing that day? Does she have braces? What color hair does she have? Then they left. I still held out hope that maybe we had a chance, maybe she was just injured, and we could handle this. It would be a tough recovery for her, but we would survive this.

Next, we were moved to a private suite inside the hospital. As I sat in that room with my ex-husband, my son, my parents, and myself, two detectives arrived to ask us some more questions. They asked for a current photo of Zoë and as I showed it to them from my phone, they looked at each other, and I knew...

They showed us a picture of a hand. Her small flawless hand with the perfectly lined French manicure and a glittery silver line right under the tips, lay lifeless on the cafeteria floor. I recognized the manicure I had taken her to get just two weeks before for her first, and last, homecoming dance. That is when they informed us that Zoë had died at the scene. My baby was dead. As I sat there in shock, unable to move, I felt a primal roar come from within my body. A rush of adrenaline and fear crashed into me with a force that was, until that day, unimaginable.

There are no words to describe how that information rang through my body. There is no sound more heart-wrenching than the sound of a mother crying out over the loss of her child. No sight as heartbreaking as a father falling to his knees in agony. A family who has just found out their child no longer breathes nor walks this earth. It broke my soul. It changed me. Everything I knew forever changed that day.

As we left the hospital suite, the hospital staff, our friends, coworkers, and community members lined the halls as a channel for us to walk through. I remember their heads bowed, hands crossed, and the outpouring of sympathy in their eyes. No one said a word. There was only silence out of respect in knowing we had lost our Zoë.

To avoid the crowd of friends, family, community members, and media, our entire family was ushered out of the hospital underground where the hospital staff had brought our vehicles so we could head home with privacy.

That ride home was long, and as we returned to the house to face our new reality; I remember everyone sitting in the same room. I didn't know what to do anymore. We all felt the simultaneous need to be together while also wanting to break off to be alone in our grief. We were all reeling from shock. Reality still had not set in. While it may seem like a strange choice, my son left the hospital with his friends. Looking back, I know that is where he needed to be. I was unable to help him or myself at that time, and it gave him a temporary sense of normalcy.

After sitting in silence for what seemed like forever, I went up to Zoë's room, and I broke. My entire body shook as I desperately clung to the pillow that still smelled of her. Hugging her pillow as I sobbed for my baby. My arms tightened around it so hard as if it were her. I imagined I had not lost her. This pillow and her room were the last closest things to her. I wanted to stay on that floor forever. I wished I never had to be there in the first place. Why wasn't anyone waking me up from this terrible nightmare?

CHAPTER 3
"ZOË" MEANS LIFE

"Zoë" Means Life

Zoë was born on February 22, 2000. It was a beautiful, crisp morning when I went to the hospital. The sun was shining, and excitement filled the air. I was ready. It was my second pregnancy, and I had less anxiety than with my first child. I was being induced and, truthfully, I couldn't wait to meet my girl!

Surrounded by family, we welcomed into this world the most beautiful baby girl I had ever seen. I can remember every detail of her sweet face – her perfectly round head, chubby little cheeks, and sweet rosebud lips. She had tiny hairs on her soft skin, and her dark brown locks were slicked down on her scalp. Everything about her was beautiful.

After having my son, I longed for a daughter. I reasoned that if I only had two children, then I would like to have one of each. As a young mother I put a lot of thought into the names of my children. I sought something uncommon. I did not want my children to have family names, nor did I want anything classic. I wanted my children to be unique from the moment I knew of their existence. I chose "Zoë" because "Zoë" means life. I chose "Raine" as her middle name, in honor of her big brother Rayden Zane.

Bringing her home completed our family. Zoë was a quiet baby, amazingly easy to please. Feed, hold, sleep, repeat. She was very content on most days. As she grew, she exhibited "leadership qualities." This is how I referred to her early streak of independence and personality. She kept everyone on their toes.

Her big brother adored her and was always ready to help hold, feed, or entertain her. The two of them were inseparable from the beginning. They had a friendship and closeness that only siblings understand. As a mother, I could not have been more overjoyed to watch their relationship grow.

Once she discovered her little raspy voice, she became a chatterbox. She would run around the house copying everything her big brother said and did. She also found her teeth, and with them the desire to bite. She would bite her brother any chance she got. Once we even captured it on video. While going through old videos I found one in which she was being extra cute for the camera. She was reciting all the words she could say and showing off her two front teeth, which we affectionately called "bucky beaver." Out of the blue, and without warning, she bit her brother on the back. I'm sure it shocked me when it happened, but I smile now when I watch that video.

Unfortunately, she thought biting was hilarious, so this was a hard habit to break. Thankfully, she eventually grew out of biting and was able to hold her own alongside her wild and crazy brother.

Zoë's love for the camera never stopped. She enjoyed having her picture taken at an early age. Of course, this was back in the early 2000s when I still had a flip phone and there was no recording or texting with that old thing.

Just before Zoë was born, I did purchase a video camera, and I am so thankful now that I have all these video memories of her early years to look back on. She loved to watch herself on video. Anytime the camera was out she would say over, and over, "I see Zoë? I see Zoë?" until I flipped the camera around so she could see herself.

Zoë seemed to grow up so fast. Perhaps it was because she was my second child, but time just flew by. On her first birthday, she wore my first birthday dress. It was sheer, light pink, with a bow on the neckline, and a flowing waistline. She wore it with white tights, white shoes, and a gold heart necklace from her great grandma. I squeezed what hair she had into a tiny pink bow, prominently on the top of her head. I remember feeling so overjoyed to pass this dress down to my daughter.

Zoë tried to open her presents before the party even began, and cried when I stopped her. She was so determined, even at that age. The theme for her party was "baby dolls," and she was thrilled that everyone brought her one. She called them "BAbums," which I enjoyed hearing her say over and over as she opened each one.

At age two, she chased after her brother, attempting all the same daredevil stunts he tried. They climbed up and down the slide in our yard, hung on with one hand, and jumped off the top steps. They raced their bikes up and down our driveway. Zoë jumped into the small kiddy pool with her diaper full of water. They jumped on and off the couch and slammed into each other until they fell over with laughter. It is a wonder no one ever broke a bone.

Around this time, we adopted some kittens. I will never forget how much Zoë loved them. I would catch her petting and trying to "cuddle" those kittens all the time and she would get so upset when I told her to leave them alone. They were not fans of her "cuddling," but she was so very tenderhearted. One day, Zoë decided to take the kittens for a ride. She put them in her booster seat, and pushed the kittens back and forth across the carpet. Those poor things had the trip of their life that day!

By three years old, Zoë had the entire family wrapped around her little finger. She grew more and more independent as the days went on. I remember her desire to get all dressed up for her third birthday party. It was a big event. We spent the evening beforehand curling her hair in those old pink foam rollers. She picked out her prettiest purple dress, shiniest shoes, and cutest hair accessories, and laid them out on her dresser in anticipation of her big day.

The next morning, she awoke with such excitement to have curly hair for the party. What she did not realize was that curly meant CURLY! After removing all the curlers, I saw the sheer look of horror on her face as she looked at her hair in the mirror. She burst into tears. Thankfully, I was able to spray it down and make it not quite as curly for her special day. Not surprisingly, she never asked for curls again.

Around this same age, Zoë began gymnastics and dance, and while she loved to do both activities, she didn't like doing them in front of other people. She tended to be a little shy when it came to the spotlight. Her first dance recital was during Christmas time, and the little ballerinas were dressed up as candy canes. She looked adorable, but she cried throughout the entire show and stood on stage without performing all the moves – you know, the typical videotaped children's dance recital. It didn't bother me, though. I just wanted my kids to experience all life has to offer, and that meant trying new things. My only requirement was that they finish out what they started. After that recital, she never went to dance class again.

Zoë thrived in preschool. She loved to go to school and bring home projects from her day. She was overjoyed to go to kinder-garten at the brand-new elementary school right down the street from our house. Going through old school papers, I found a rainbow with her picture attached. Zoë's teacher had written out questions for each color of the rainbow, e.g.: *What is your favorite color?* Zoë colored the first row in the rainbow with her favorite color; pink. The second row was blue; the color of her eyes. Peach for the color of her skin. Brown for the color of her hair. Red for the color of her favorite food (strawberries).

Zoë loved rainbows, and it is only fitting that I feel her pres-ence every time I see one. Rainbows reinforce for me that signs and spirit are all around us. You just need to be open to receiving and interpreting them.

When the kids were growing up, we lived in a cul-de-sac, in a nice cookie-cutter neighborhood, with the best neighbors. We were fortunate to have neighbors that we would sit out front with while the kids played. Zoë had two little friends, Cheyenne and Bryttanie, that were the same age. The girls had so much fun together. I remember them performing together in my living room. Sometimes it was dance recitals, and other times it was gymnastic routines. They laughed endlessly as they flung themselves around on the hardwood floors. They were always so full of life and laughter. I often think of this particular memory when I look back at Zoë's life.

Zoë was a friend to everyone. She always enjoyed her friends, even at an early age. After she died, I received messages from parents telling me how wonderful she had been to their children. One parent said that Zoë wrote the sweetest note in their child's yearbook and that note made her child's day. Another parent stated Zoë was a kind soul that befriended their child at a time when no one else had. It touched me to know that she was perceived as a kind soul to others, and that she had positively touched the lives of her peers.

My husband and I were regularly active, and our children inherited this trait early on. By four years old, Zoë participated in gymnastics and biddy sports at the local YMCA. She loved soccer, and made it her recreation of choice. She played all-year-round on a great team in her little number four, teal jersey. She and her brother both played soccer, which made our days full of games. Zoë made so many friends while playing soccer, and was ecstatic when her best friend, Paige, joined her team.

In middle school, Zoë played volleyball, tried out for Softball, and was a wrestling team manager. She also participated in our local gym. We loved going to the gym as a family, and our gym family has continued to love and support us through the years. They have since dedicated an annual workout in honor of the victims of the high school shooting, which they run on the anniversary of Zoë's death. Each year, so many people send me pictures from the event, showing their continued love and support.

From an early age, Zoë had such a mindful way of looking at the world. She always pushed the boundaries with her inquisitive nature. She frequently dumbfounded me with her insightful questions. She and her dad would have conversations about life. She was a gifted conversationalist. She was growing into such a strong, independent woman. I often think about the impact that her incredible mind could have had on this world, and it saddens me.

Zoë had a zest for life. She enjoyed music, going to live concerts, and allowed herself to let go and really feel her surroundings. She loved animals and her heart was pure. I believe she could have been so many things in life but her true nature was that of a caregiver. Sometimes I picture her as a doctor, nurse, or veterinarian.

Zoë had a great sense of humor, and she loved to laugh. She had a laugh that I still hear every day – a contagious, loud, and unrestrained laugh that pulled you in. She found humor in so many things. After Zoë died, Paige's mom emailed me a video that she had found on her computer. It is one of the greatest videos, and the longest video I have of Zoë as a teenager. She and Paige were playing the game "Chubby Bunny" and as they sat there filming themselves, they laughed, giggled, snorted, and cried tears of happiness as they stuffed their mouths with marshmallows.

That video is the perfect reminder of what a fun, charismatic girl she was. It reminds me of her innocence, her fun-loving nature, and how she was just starting to see the world. It is a joyful memory, but a painful reminder of my loss and the fact that my daughter should be here living carefree, and full of laughter.

Have you found things from the person you lost that you didn't realize existed until years later? Recently, I came across over two-thousand photos and videos from Zoë's old iPod. What a trip down memory lane for me. I found photos and videos of her enjoying life that I had never seen before. She laughed and joked with her friends, still in the innocence of childhood. What an amazing treasure to find. Finding these new photos and videos, after years of thinking I'd never have anything more of her, gave me the energy to keep writing her story.

One of the last trips we went on as a family was to Disney-land. We took the kids there every other year since Zoë was four. My kids loved thrill rides. They would spend hours riding all the rides and enjoying everything about "the greatest place on Earth." When she was younger, Zoë always looked forward to dressing up as a princess and getting the autographs of all the princess characters in the park. Zoë was carefree and innocent, with the entire world in front of her.

One of my favorite moments from all of our Disney adventures was the time we sat outside the Haunted Mansion ride where the large fountain displays the Fantasia show in the evenings. Zoë had on her princess dress, her face was painted, and her hair a mess from a day full of joy rides. She twirled and twirled as the colors danced in the background. Those blessed memories help fill the void when I ache deeply for my daughter.

The summer before Zoë died, we took a trip to California. We enjoyed beach time, boogie boarding, and henna tattoos. I remember thinking how amazing it was spending time enjoying life now that the kids were older. I felt that the teenage years were not going to be that bad. My kids were becoming very opinionated, but very cool independent adults.

When Zoë was thirteen, she fell in love for the first time. My heart swelled knowing that the first teenage love is the one you always remember. Even if you have other loves in lifetime, you never forget your first one. I am forever grateful that she got to experience young love in her brief lifetime. When she died, she was dating a handsome young man and their love was blossoming as they spent more time together. Unfortunately, he also died in the senseless tragedy that took my girl.

Zoë and I had many mother-daughter dates through the years. I started taking her to get her mini mani-pedis as early as age three. She loved to pick out the polish color, and she sat so well for the ladies. As she got older, we started our nail days with coffee. We loved our weekly trips to the drive-through coffee stand by our house. The baristas knew our order and it was always ready when we arrived.

Zoë's first homecoming dance was the week before she died. We went dress shopping and found the perfect diamond-accented black dress, and fancy, strappy sandals. On the day of the dance, we shared girl time. We got coffees and prepped her for the big event. She wanted me to do her hair and requested a waterfall braid with curls on the ends. She also asked for a smoky eye look and, thankfully, I was able to pull it off.

As she sat on the floor in front of the mirror, finishing her makeup, we hung out like any mother and daughter would. We talked about how nervous she was to go to the dance, and how excited she felt all at the same time. We talked about who was dating whom and all the latest gossip in her world. Looking back, I am grateful I took the opportunity to calm her fears, and listen without judgment.

I wish I could turn back time. The day was so beautiful, and my girl was stunning. As I took photos of her, I could tell she was still a little nervous. She kept asking me how she looked. My response was, "You are always so beautiful."

I have so many memories of our special times together, and treasure how comfortable she felt with me that we could have those open conversations. I long for the days we had together. I miss the woman that she was becoming, our precious relationship, and the life we shared. I miss my best friend.

"Zoë" means life and, even though she is no longer with us earth side, her presence is always around us. Her zest for life, her exuberant smile, and her infectious laugh are memories that will never fade away. Beautiful memories of her in happier times, are tucked away in those videos I have saved. I get to hear her voice, see her move, and listen to her laugh. All that I have left of my beautiful girl are the memories. I am so thankful for the preserved moments of her living her best life, forever fourteen.

CHAPTER 4
THE FUNERAL

This next chapter may read something like a thank you letter, but I feel it is necessary to acknowledge the importance of community in overcoming tragedy. As this book is meant to help you move through your grief, I cannot stress enough how vital it is to build a community of support before tragedy strikes. Since we never know when, or if, our lives will suddenly be turned upside down, start building your community today. Be a good friend. Be a coworker that others can count on. Be active in your community, and a force for good. Pick up others when they are down. Because it will be these same people that will have your back when your life is in pieces. I know that was certainly the case for us after Zoë's death.

The days after Zoë's death were a whirlwind. I was clearly in a state of shock and denial. My world became very overwhelming very quickly. Even small decisions were difficult for me, and most days were a blur. It felt like one of those scenes in a movie where I stared blankly through teary eyes while the rest of the world hustled and bustled around me. Everything was in slow motion, but I couldn't understand how everyone, and everything kept going when my world had come to a crashing halt.

There is nothing that prepares you for making funeral preparations for a child. This was a difficult process, and we decided to have Zoë cremated due to the nature of her injury. Also due to the nature of her injury, we were prevented from seeing her after her death. This has been one of many difficult factors for me – one that repeatedly came up in therapy. Not seeing her lifeless body prevented me from having any sense of closure. The detectives told me my daughter died at the scene. They showed me her lifeless hand in a photo. But that is all. When the coroner's office called me, I assumed we would go down and identify her body. But they told me I could not come, and that her Orthodontist would need to come down and provide dental records for identification.

How do you move forward when you are only *told* your daughter died? When you can't kiss her cheek one last time? Without the visual proof that your precious child is no longer in this world? The first few years I struggled with this immensely, and it hurt me to my core. Looking back now, I can appreciate that my last images of her are happy ones, with her infectious laugh and beautiful smile. That is how she should be remembered.

A few days before her body was cremated. I wrote her a three-page letter to be placed with her before cremation. I told her all the wonderful things that she taught me in life, and I reminisced over the fond memories I had of us together. I told her that I would always honor her memory and would use it to move forward in life and make this world a better place. I asked her to watch over her father and brother and help guide them through their pain. I also told her how much she meant to us all. This was the only way I gained a sense of closure.

I am eternally grateful to my friends Ginny and Mariah for taking the reins and making Zoë's funeral arrangements. Neither skipped a beat as they made all the decisions from the colors, decorations, pamphlets, and food. They even organized a downline of friends and community members to help. To everyone that stepped in to help, I hope you know how grateful I am to you all.

Washington State Crime Victims Compensation Program covered some transportation and hotel expenses for out-of-state family, and helped with anything else that we needed. My dearest friend, Erika, used her position at an airline to organize airline tickets for my out of state family and friends. Having them at the funeral was such a comfort to me, and I am so grateful for Erika's role.

My friend, Vicki, spoke on behalf of the family. Zoë's friends, Paige and Julisa, took the stand to speak in her honor. Rayden, never ceasing to amaze me with his strength, created a beautiful playlist for the funeral, filled with many songs that they shared a love for. It was such a loving tribute to his sister. My friend, Mariah, put together a beautiful slide show of Zoë with the playlist. So many precious memories were shared that day

Word of Life Lutheran Brethren Church provided musicians and the reception location. Local police effectively navigated the large number of people flooding in for the funeral, and kept the media away. So many friends, family, community members, and military servicemembers attended.

I never imagined how hard it would be to do even the simplest thing in the wake of Zoë's death. Getting dressed for her funeral was difficult. I didn't want to leave my bed, but I knew I needed to pull myself together, show up, and say my final farewell. While black is traditional funeral attire, Rayden and I both wore teal as a nod to Zoë's favorite color. This color has become permanently entwined with Zoë's memory, as it was the color of her funeral decorations as well.

I stood at the front of the church as a line of people that extended past the back of the church came up to hug and console my family one by one. I stood on numb feet, feeling as though I would black out at any moment. What I remember most are the faces of everyone grieving our loss with us. We knew we were not alone in our grief.

We placed a headstone for her at the Marysville Cemetery and spread some of her ashes there. It has been a wonderful place for the community to come and pay their respects. Zoë had touched so many lives over the years, I felt it necessary to give her a space within the community that loved and supported her so much.

CHAPTER 5
NEVER GREW UP

My Zoë stopped at fourteen years old. She would never again have any firsts. No more homecoming dances. No wedding day. No first-time motherhood. I grieved the loss of our future daily phone conversations, and the advice I would offer her when she faced life's challenges. A piece of our family was gone too soon.

Although the trauma of losing Zoë has softened, I feel heartache for her every day. I start and end my days looking at her picture and saying her name. Random things throughout my day will remind me of her, and I find comfort thinking about things she enjoyed in life.

Zoë was an artist with a vision beyond her years. The artistic influences of my mother, Zoë's father, and Rayden fueled her passion. When Zoë was twelve, her love for animals came through in her art. She perfectly captured the likenesses of our old black and white lab, George, and our cat Bella. She made a beautiful drawing of a koi fish for a middle school art room project, and it overjoys me to see the beauty she saw in the world through her art.

The meaning of one of Zoë's drawings gained significance after her death. She drew a picture of Peter Pan, with the caption, "Never Grow Up." The picture impacted me so deeply, that I had it turned into a memorial tattoo in honor of her. It turned out perfect, and in an appropriate twist of fate, the "o" in "grow" sometimes looks like an "e," making the phrase "Never Grew Up." It is a daily reminder that although she didn't grow up, her art continues to impact others.

Prior to Zoë's death she was sketching regularly, and I stumbled upon multiple works in progress. One of her most famous expressions of art is a poster-sized "Make Love, Not War" piece. She took hours to hand draw the peace sign in the middle using a filigree style. She even included small messages inside the filigree, only visible on close inspection, and her name is hidden throughout. The original is a cherished piece and hangs proudly in our home. It was also used as part of a fundraiser for the students affected by the tragedy. A local company put student artwork on T-Shirts which were then sold to collect money for the school's student recovery fund. I was extremely proud to be able to honor her in this way. The shirts gave the students a piece of Zoë to hold on to, and gave me some comfort in those early days.

CHAPTER 6
FORGIVENESS IN THE AFTERMATH

There was no way for me to prepare for the emptiness that set in when things started to settle down after the funeral. It happened when all of the out-of-town family headed back home, fewer people stopped by to pay their respects, and the many flowers we received, died. The once vibrant and colorful flowers dried up, the water became brown, and the leaves fell off the stems. It was symbolic of how I felt inside. The condolence cards were piled up, waiting to be read, and all of the leftover food went untouched because I just couldn't eat. I often sat in silence, not knowing what I was supposed to do next.

After going through this very public tragedy, everyone wanted a piece of me. In less than twenty-four hours after the tragedy occurred, I was inundated with media requests. Everyone was eager to be the first one to get the inside scoop, but I had yet to process what was happening and the last thing I needed was media attention. You would be appalled at some of the requests I received. I was even asked for permission to film her funeral!

But my experience is, unfortunately, not unique. When tragedy strikes, everyone wants all the juicy details. Everyone wants to be involved in some way. People are drawn in like flies to a flame when a tragedy occurs. While many people are genuinely kind and sympathetic, many are agenda-driven and profit-seeking. I get it – it is human nature to be curious and drawn to drama. But it is absolutely traumatic to be in the middle of the worst trial of your life, being hounded from every direction.

I came in contact with everyone from conspiracy theorists who believed that it was all a political stunt with no real victims, to "grief seekers" who prey on people during times of pain. I was not prepared for the grief seekers. These are either people you do not know or people that you have not spoken to in years, that heard about the tragic event and want to somehow be connected to it. At first, they may seem helpful and harmless, so you allow them in. But it often felt like they wanted the tragedy to drag on, and they thrived seeing me at my lowest. If I was not offering up enough sadness, anger, or self-destruction, then it was as if they were trying to create more for me. Moving forward was not on their agenda, and it always felt they were trying to hold me back from healing. What is difficult with grief seekers is their need for you to continue to live in the pain. Not one of those people is still around today, they have all gone and moved onto someone else's tragedy.

Many of the issues I encountered were on social media. I received an incredible amount of online bashing including private messages with derogatory content about who I was as a parent. Learning to find boundaries for this took some time and a quick "block" here and there and it was usually over with. It hurt my heart to know that these people exist and that they would seek to further hurt me during the most difficult time in my life.

As you can probably imagine, there were many opportunists that bombarded me after Zoë's death. Some people tried to use her memory to financially benefit themselves, or to gain social media popularity. It was traumatic to have to fiercely defend my daughter's memory when I hadn't even gotten used to the idea of her being gone. Fortunately, the vast majority of people that came to help were angels on Earth, and selflessly stepped in where they were needed. I will never be able to give enough thanks to those who helped so we could pay our bills, take time off work, and mourn.

A few weeks after Zoë's death, I decided it was time to share my story. I finally allowed my story to be told by a wonderful reporter, named Alex. His request for an interview stood out because it was heartfelt, compassionate, and his words spoke to me. I knew he was the one to tell my story.

The first time we met was over coffee and he listened with his whole heart. There were no microphones, no cameras, no notepads – it was just us sitting in a café like two old friends. We talked about who Zoë was, as a way to try to bring some light to this tragedy. When we finally scheduled the cameras, it was a difficult interview and I second-guessed myself every step of the way. Alex and his team did a wonderful job. They were kind and compassionate and made sure I was comfortable with the story before it aired. I hoped that by giving the interview, I'd be left alone by the rest of the media. Unfortunately, I was wrong, it took about a year for the attention to calm down.

My main goal in doing the interview was to share Zoë's memory, and to tell the world that I forgave her shooter. It was hard to say aloud that I forgive him. When everyone else was still angry, somehow, I was able to see the hurting child behind the horrendous act. I mourned for his lost childhood, and I mourned for his mother that lost her child. I was not the only one hurting in this situation.

Unfortunately, it seems that today's teens do not fully understand the consequences of their actions. Many children do not possess the coping skills to manage daily stressors in the current world we live in. How can we change this? Not a day goes by that I don't wonder what could have been done differently in this boy's life to alter his path to destruction.

What a sad world that we live in when a child sees death as their only option. Where are we failing our children? Many people disagreed with my decision to forgive him. Many family members were angry and couldn't understand my decision. What they did not understand was that by forgiving Zoë's murderer, I was able to move forward in my grief. As I moved forward, I witnessed other family members become "stuck" in their anger.

Holding onto anger would not allow me to take the action that I needed to find out what happened to my child. Moving forward with the police and FBI to find out what caused this tragic event needed my full attention and holding onto anger prevented me from focusing.

Before the shooting I was already going through some complicated life changes. I knew I was not being the best parent I could be. My husband and I were going through a divorce, our children were both struggling to process it. He and I were both admittedly on parenting autopilot as we focused on our dissolving marriage. As a parent, I want to provide the best life that I can for my children. Life usually does not work out the way we plan. Although I have many regrets from that time, I have grown from my mistakes, and learned to accept what I cannot change.

The first two years were the hardest emotionally and physically for me. Grieving the loss of my daughter, broke me. As a fitness professional, I knew exercise would help with the depression and anxiety I was feeling. Unfortunately, I was not able to motivate myself in my grief, and instead, I let old bad habits, like smoking, creep back in. How could I coach athletes, run marathons, and promote a healthy lifestyle while I was not taking care of myself and was secretly smoking in the background? I felt like I had zero control over anything in my life. I was just trying to make it through each day. Survival mode looks differently for all of us, and there is no shame in it.

I also tried going to therapy for a while after Zoë's death. That early therapy was largely unsuccessful for me because I was nowhere near ready to do the hard work and emotional digging that it required. It was just too soon and too difficult. The feelings of guilt, the wish that your life would have been taken instead of your child's. How do you tell someone that you want to die? My deepest, darkest thoughts were just too much to share with another person. It scares me to look back at how I felt almost six years ago.

Although, it is impossibly challenging when your child is ripped away in circumstances outside of your control, and the multitude of emotions, thoughts, and decisions that you go through will frighten you, you can overcome them and you will emerge stronger. I promise!

My journey was normal, I see that now. As a mother, I am the caregiver, the glue that holds my family together. I protect and sacrifice everything I can so that my children can thrive. When things get in the way of that, it is easy to feel as though we have failed. I prided myself on my strength and tenacity to face whatever the world could throw at me, so coming to my breaking point, and letting people in to help pick up the pieces was incredibly difficult for me. But my son saved me from myself as a teenager and he saved me again during this tragic time. He is the only reason I was able to move forward, the reason I ditched the bad habits and began to become healthy again. I knew that he deserved better.

My message to anyone finding themselves in the dark place after the loss of a child is to recognize that in time, and with hope, you will find your way. You will adjust to a new normal. Take the time you need, go easy on yourself, and allow others to comfort you. Good people greatly outweigh the negative people after a tragedy. They will be ready to jump in and help pick up the pieces when you can't. Let them.

CHAPTER 7
FINDING JOY AFTER PAIN

To combat the pain, I was feeling after losing Zoë, I veered toward replacing the numbness caused by emotional pain with physical pain. It was an indescribable need to feel something – anything. When you experience an emotional trauma so severe, it is difficult for any competing emotion to even register for a long time. Physical pain allowed me to feel again, even if it was still an unpleasant sensation. And for me, at that time, it was something different than my grief, and I'd choose anything over my grief. As I sat for my first tattoo after Zoë died, I remember telling the artist to take his time, I was in no rush. I wanted to feel every puncture of the needle. But still, nothing removed my grief, so I started to self-medicate.

I had experienced the relief of anti-depressants from post-partum depression after the birth of my son, so I sought that relief again. In the early days, I cannot even tell you what I was given, as I was open to whatever someone put in my hand. Thankfully, my sister in law works in the medical field and she stepped in, contacted my doctor, and got me set up with the proper medications. I had medication for sleeping, medication to "pick me up" during the day, and an anti-depressant. There were many days that I took them all and still wanted something stronger. I had some leftover muscle relaxers and pain medication from a past back issue, and I took them. I was also smoking cigarettes and drinking alcohol.

This is how I coped that entire first year. I do experience some amount of shame to admit all of my substance use, but it was a real part of my journey. If you find yourself here, please know, you are not alone. But I encourage you to seek professional help as self-medicating can quickly become dangerous and out of your control. Coping mechanisms come in many different forms. The important part is to remember that help is available, and you will benefit from seeking it out.

Shortly before Zoë died, I had started dating a wonderful man. While many marriages don't last through tragedy, my boyfriend chose to stay the course through everything. I gave him so many reasons to leave, but I am so grateful that he chose to stay. Two years later, we were making plans to get married. A few months before we got married, I decided to ween off all my prescribed medications, and the cigarettes. I knew after we were married, we would be trying for a baby. I had to get back to wellness. This altered state could not stay my new normal. I needed to move forward.

I got sober, and I married the love of my life, and within a few months, we found out we were expecting a baby girl, and we'd be moving to a different state as a result of my new husband's job in the military. As hard as it was to think about leaving my son and my family, I knew we needed this fresh start. No one would know me or my story. I wouldn't dread trips to the store, and I wouldn't have to brace myself for the glances I received. I wouldn't be immediately thought of as the woman whose daughter was murdered in the school shooting. I would be able to walk with my head up again. It was my chance at a new identity, away from the place that held nothing but reminders of Zoë's absence.

After we moved, I felt a sense of peace and calm. I could finally breathe again, and my anxiety lessened. I embraced the prospect of making new friends, and not being immediately associated with the tragedy. I would be able to choose who knew my story, and I felt a refreshing sense of control over my story.

Moving away gave me a fresh start to work on myself, and to learn how to navigate this new life. It also provided me with some much-needed clarity. I went back to counseling, and it has been a huge asset to my well-being. I found a great counselor that I share a wonderful connection with, and she has been such an important part of my journey to wellness.

Shortly after we moved, we welcomed our beautiful baby girl,
Lotte. Having a child after a loss is a rollercoaster of
emotions. I wondered if I could love another child. Would I
be well enough to care for her? When we found out we were
having a girl, I cried tears of guilt *and* happiness. Guilt
because I wanted a boy so that I would not have to love
another little girl. I felt as though it would be extremely difficult to love another girl after losing Zoë, and that I would
constantly compare them. I somehow felt loving another
daughter would betray Zoë's memory, but simultaneously I
felt an overwhelming sense of happiness that I was being
given another chance to raise another beautiful girl.

I second-guessed every feeling that I had, and wondered how
it would be possible to ever feel joy and peace again. I worried
about being judged if I shared a photo of myself smiling. I
wondered if people would think I was "over it." I constantly
wondered, "What is the *right* behavior? Friends, there is no
right. There is just moving forward.

CHAPTER 8
ZOË LIVES ON

Zoë loved to play dress up as a small child. While she loved everything girly, she also loved playing in the mud with her brother. She was tough – she had to be - her brother was an animal in the way that most little boys are. Rayden has always been the jokester of the family, and he loved to push Zoë just enough to get a rise out of her. They were the best of friends and had the sibling love that every parent wants for their children. Every Christmas Eve, Zoë and Rayden would sleep in the same room. One year, Zoë woke up sick, and projectile-vomited all over her brother and his room, but he still allowed the sleepover the next year simply because it was their tradition.

Zoë with Rayden used to jump for hours on the trampoline together. In the rain, in the snow and with a sprinkler underneath. They built forts under it and had secret conversations no one else was privy to. I would watch them from the deck and just appreciate the relationship they had. They were always laughing and joking, and if one got their feelings hurt or a disagreement arose, they fixed it themselves.

When Zoë died, a piece of Rayden left with her. He lost his best friend. But one thing that I have noticed over the years is people have come into both of our lives that remind us of her. Rayden's fiancé, Miya, is a beautiful girl, filled with so much kindness, and parts of her remind me of Zoë. She has made such an impact on Rayden, and it is evident that she completes him. She has become his new best friend to walk with for the rest of his life.

My medium came into my life early on, and has provided me with pieces of Zoë that help keep my heart fulfilled. Sometimes it is through an acknowledgment of what I am doing or an old memory that Zoë sends me. I appreciate all the visions that I am given. They always show up at the right times, and provide me such a sense of overall calmness when I am in need.

As my little Lotte grows, I see so many traits of Zoë in her. She most definitely has a personality of her own, but now and then she brings a little bit of Zoë to me, and it brings my heart peace. Lotte has the same hair color, texture, part, and double cowlick that Zoë had. Lotte shares her big sister's beautiful blue eyes, and she, too, loves to dress up and do her makeup and look at herself in the same pink mirror that was once Zoë's. Lotte has a little bit of Zoë's "leadership" spunk which has earned her the nickname "Boss Baby", reminiscent of Zoë's nickname, "Bossy Galasso."

Some days I just look at Lotte and feel so thankful to be allowed to have a second chance at all the mother-daughter experiences that I didn't get to continue with Zoë. When I used to think about never seeing Zoë walk down the aisle or as a new mother, I felt so much sadness. But now, I find restored hope that I will experience them with Lotte. It will never be the same, for Lotte is not a replacement, but it will be a wonderful experience with beautiful similarities as I carry Zoë's memory with me through them.

Zoë, you will never be forgotten. I cherish every single reminder of you, and it brings me so much joy knowing your spirit still lives on.

CHAPTER 9
SEARCHING FOR ANSWERS

In my journey through grief, I spent a lot of time searching for answers. I became fixated on finding out exactly what happened to Zoë, and I struggled knowing that I didn't have all the information. I felt like I needed to know exactly what happened to my daughter. As in any situation, the only people that know exactly what took place are those present and directly involved. Any information I received was either secondhand or concluded based on evidence gathered at the scene. I found that certain small bits of information, that seemed insignificant at first, would come back and haunt me later, after I had time to process it. I grasped at any scrap of information that made me feel connected to her or offered me some closure.

This is how I found myself going to psychics. For a while, I was spending money for information I already knew. Generic platitudes like, "Your loved one is at peace and she wants you to be happy." It was stuff that *anyone* could tell me, and these people were more charlatans than clairvoyants. One woman wanted almost $500 to enroll me in a "healing program" before she'd be able to give me more information. I walked out!

Despite my initial negative experiences, I still believed that some people had the gift of communicating with spirits, so I continued my search. I know the idea of using mediums is unsavory to some, and doesn't align with everyone's belief system, and I am not saying that it is the only way to get closure. I'm merely saying that it worked for me, and it has helped me move forward, and that is the most important thing to me.

Theresa Caputo, a.k.a. The Long Island Medium, has a television show where she does readings on audience members. Some of my good friends, and some of the other victims' mothers went to her show in the hopes that she'd do a reading on us. We sat two rows back from the stage and watched in awe. We held our breath, and with sweaty palms, watched as she read the people in front of us and the people next to us, but unfortunately, she did not read us that day.

Encouraged by what I saw at the show, I called a local medium, Terri, who's information had been given to me early on. Interestingly, she had also attended the Theresa Caputo show, and had a vision on her way home that I was going to be contacting her. Terri answered the phone and said, "I knew you were going to call me." She gave me a few answers right over the phone and I booked my first session with her. I felt encouraged.

I met with Terri in June of 2015, and although I initially felt nervous that I was on another dead-end mission, I was immediately put at ease. Terri lives on a beautiful, serene property. It is a lovely place for healing, and it allowed me to be open and receptive. Terri and I sat down in her "Zen room" and immediately, Zoë came to her. Zoë's presence was palpable. I could feel her laughter. Terri quickly put any of my skepticism to rest when she brought forth memories of Zoë's childhood that only I would know.

Zoë showed Terri visions of herself dressed up and having a tea party. She spoke about the tea set itself and how it looked, even detailing the princess dress and tiara she was wearing. She even showed Terri where she was shot, which I later confirmed with the coroner's report.

Terri brought through a vision of Zoë's Grammy creating a magnificent garden in Zoë's honor. I later found out this possibly had happened *while* I was having my reading. Terri was able to see the small angels my mom had put on all the children's gravesites. I laughed when Terri asked, "I am seeing plastic hamster balls rolling around and cats chasing them across wood. Do you know what this means?" I laughed, and I said, "My kids had hamsters and our cats used to bat the hamster balls around on our hardwood floors." She then said, "I see honey or syrup or something sweet going along with this. Please tell me I am not losing my mind!" I smiled and told her the hamster's name was "Maple" like the syrup.

Terri also saw my marriage, and a baby coming. She said I would have a girl, and she was correct. This time with Terri was one of the most magical experiences I have ever had. It provided the closure I craved and brought me a sense of indescribable peace.

After my reading with Terri, my grief changed. I found I could move forward toward healing, and could start to honor Zoë in the way she deserved. This reading gave me hope, after months of feeling broken beyond repair, and I finally felt strength returning to me.

To this day, Terri is a good friend and she checks in with me often. Sometimes, during our chats, Zoë will chime in and that always brings me back to that first reading, and the happiness that it provided for me. They're like little reminders that she is okay and that I can continue onward with my healing journey.

CHAPTER 10
SPIRITUAL PATH TO PEACE

G rief impacts us physically, emotionally, cognitively, socially, and spiritually. Losing someone you love, no matter the cause, can make us feel as though we are being ripped apart. To fully heal, I believe we need to address all of these areas.

On the day that Zoë died, I received many calls from friends, telling me they were praying for me, for Zoë, and for our family. Although I've tried, I truly don't understand how prayer works. I asked for prayers, and I even prayed as we drove to the hospital. I spoke to the sky and asked God to save Zoë. I sat in the hospital waiting room saying over and over in my head, "I will believe in you, if you just save my baby." But God did not answer me in the way that I wanted. Looking back, I wonder if he ignored my prayers because I had never believed in him. I've wondered if pushing religion aside during my teenage years was to blame. Was my daughter taken from me because I chose to believe something else? Logic tells me no, of course not. But I struggled with this for a long time.

I was brought up to believe in the God of the Bible. I grew up Catholic, went to Catechism classes, and participated in youth group. As a teenager, I ventured out to churches of different denominations with friends. But I could never truly wrap my brain around what we were doing, and why we were doing it. Perhaps I was too young. Maybe, I did not like the required church attendance. I really don't know what it was, but I never "got it." As an adult I choose not to go to church. I've never had a relationship with God, so I just don't make Him a part of my life.

Maybe you, too, have asked God, "Why?" a thousand times, and never felt you've been given a satisfactory response. You may feel alone and unheard because nothing you did could prevent the loss of your loved one. Please know that you are not alone in questioning yourself and questioning God during this time. I have confidence that you will return to your destined path in your own time. I am still exploring my own spiritual path. I still question and feel doubt. I believe there is an energy in this world, maybe that is God, maybe not. I believe that everyone is entitled to their own belief system, and I don't believe there are any right or wrong answers. I believe in good, and in kindness, and I try to live every day with good intent, and goodwill toward others. If I succeed in my efforts to serve humanity, then I have peace. We all need to take the time to find our own spiritual path toward healing.

CHAPTER 11
SIGNS EVERYWHERE

When people leave this world, I believe their energy still exists. Starting right after Zoë's death, I started to experience a number of strange things that had seemingly no explanation. While some people may say I was grasping at things to hold on to, I believe that Zoë was trying to communicate with us in this way. If you've ever experienced something like this, then you know what I'm talking about.

One of the first signs I experienced after Zoë's death was what we refer to as "the yellow stopwatch occurrence." I had been using a yellow stopwatch at work for years, and never in all of my years using this stopwatch did it ever go off on its own. After Zoë passed, this stopwatch went off randomly for days, and I could not turn it off no matter how hard or how many times I pushed the buttons. It just continued to beep and beep and beep. After days of this, the watch stopped just as suddenly as it started. It hasn't made a sound since, and now sits silently in a chest full of her items. To add another layer of intrigue to this, some homemade blankets from a local church's women's group were dropped off, and one of them was covered in racecars and yellow stopwatches!

There seemed to be quite a number of "power surges" surrounding Zoë's family that first week after her death. Her dad's dryer turned itself on randomly throughout the day and night, even after he checked all of the settings. My husband, Simon, had a solar watch that stopped that entire week too, and no matter how much light we gave it, it would not turn back on. The next week, it was running back to normal and to this day still runs without issue. Zoë's grandparent's computer would randomly turn itself on and off during that time period too. The disk drive started popping in and out on its own at all hours of the day and night, but it has never happened since.

My seven-month-old nephew would wake up crying in the middle of the night and, through the monitor, my brother and sister-in-law would watch him look up, smile and slowly fall back to sleep. Zoë loved her little cousin so much and we believe she was visiting him and calming him back to sleep.

After the dust had settled and it was time to go through Zoë's things, I received another sign. She and I had matching mother/daughter necklaces, like the best friend necklaces that you find at your local mall. I searched everywhere for her half of the necklace, and it was nowhere to be found. I looked in her jewelry box and drawers' numerous times to no avail. It wasn't in her items I received back from the police department, either. Finally one day, as I went to search again, I opened her jewelry box, and it was neatly sitting right in the front, with chain wrapped around it as if it had been placed there deliberately for me to see. There is no way I would have missed it in my previous searches. I will never know how it returned to the jewelry box, but I like to believe that she put it there. Sadly, this same necklace set hung around my rear-view mirror for years, and somehow, I misplaced it while cleaning my car. I hold onto hope that she will deliver it back to me again someday.

After losing her necklace, I was looking for something to have in my vehicle in honor of her, and I came across a personalized visor clip that read, "never drive faster than your guardian angel can fly." I went through the entire process to purchase but decided against it at the last minute. A few weeks later, the visor clip arrived in the mail. I wondered if I had accidentally purchased it after all. I wouldn't entirely put it past myself to do so, but I was quite sure I had not. The note inside was from my friend Angie, and it said, "I saw this and knew you needed to have it."

Once, my son and I went away for a weekend together at my friend Shari's beautiful beach house on one of the nearby local islands. As we walked along the beach together, we found a perfectly heart-shaped rock and knew this was a sign from her. There have been so many signs throughout the years, that I have a hard time believing they are all coincidences.

I also had many dreams and nightmares in the first few months after Zoë died. One night I had the sensation of someone grabbing my leg, and I awoke in sheer terror. The entire room felt full of negative energy. It was one of the strangest experiences I have ever encountered. While I'm sure some of my dreams were brought on by the amount of stress I was enduring, I do believe some were meant to ease my mind. One of my most calming dreams happened while I was in Virginia visiting a friend. I woke up as the entire guest room became illuminated. My senses were heightened in that moment, and it was as if I could smell Zoë and feel her presence. An overall sense of peace surrounded me like a warm blanket. The experience lasted a few minutes, and I will never forget the serenity of it. I just knew it was from Zoë. I cannot explain it any other way. I still don't know if the experience was real or merely a dream, but I do believe she wanted to let me know she was alright, and that I would be alright too.

After that experience, my dreams became fewer and farther apart. Now, when I dream of Zoë, I may see glimpses of her smiling, or she may make a brief appearance, but the dreams feel more like normal dreams. I like to think of them as her checking-in with me.

Everyone who knows our story associates Zoë with rainbows. To this day, I am often sent or tagged in rainbow photos. I love when this happens, as it reinforces the community that has continued to support us over the years. It brings a smile to my face and serves as a positive reminder that people continue to remember and honor Zoë. On the day she died; a rainbow could be seen over the school. In the days following the shooting, there were rainbow sightings over the hospital as well.

In those first few months, rainbows greeted me everywhere. I'd frequently see them outside of my work and my house. When Rayden hiked the same trail, we went on during our last hike with Zoë, he saw the most beautiful rainbow as he came into a clearing. My friend and neighbor had faith in me to write this book to honor Zoë, and the week I decided to get serious and do it, she called me outside of the house to see the most beautiful double rainbow stretched over our homes. I knew that this was Zoë's way of showing her approval for me to move forward.

CHAPTER 12
FOREVER CHANGED

After Zoë's death, I had to come to terms with how my life would forever be different. I would never get back to "normal." The ramifications of losing Zoë seep into every aspect of my life in some way or another, even to this day. Tragedy in any form changes a person. My family dynamic was forever altered. Friendships took on a different weight. I'm less resilient to stressors and I don't have the emotional energy for things like I used to. I'm constantly just the slightest trigger away from a post-traumatic stress episode. I know that saying these things doesn't paint the brightest picture of hope, but what it does is open your eyes to the reality that your reality will be different. The sooner you can embrace that fact, the better you will fare.

When death is sudden and unexpected, adjusting to the loss can be more difficult because there was no time to process the loss, pre-tragedy. One day you are enjoying each other's company and the next they are gone. In addition to grief, your body is also processing shock. It was so difficult not to get lost in my own grief, and to remember that the rest of my family was also suffering. They were all going through a multitude of emotions alongside me. I had to remember that my family members were crumbling with me. It was difficult to navigate the different ways in which each family member handled their shock and grief. When we were not on the same page, it was important to be gentle with everyone as best as I could. This dynamic made grieving feel so lonely and isolating. Everyone needed their own timeline to heal, to accept and understand what has happened, and to process what they were going through.

My son grieved in his own way, as he should, and I felt so bad that I could not be there for him in the way that he wanted or needed. He kept his distance, and internalized his pain, which worried me immensely. I worried that he would head down the wrong path and look to destroying his life, rather than overcome his grief. Teenage years are difficult even without experiencing the tragedy of losing a sibling or friend, so to endure a tragic loss during this time would cause any teen to lose their way. But Rayden is strong and resilient. He persevered through this into a strong, reliable young man. Like me, he is forever changed but he is thriving. He honors Zoë by doing and seeing all that she could not. He is a survivor, and I am so proud of the man he has become.

What I was not prepared for, was the extent to which this effected my parents. My parents love whole-heartedly, and they love their grandbabies with all their being, so of course something like this wouldn't be easy for them. But losing Zoë devastated their world. I have never seen my parents so broken, in all my years watching them tackle life and all its obstacles. At times, I worried they would not survive Zoë's death, and as I grieved for the loss of my daughter, I began to feel that I would lose my parents as well. It was exceedingly difficult to see the hurt that overtook them emotionally and physically. It has certainly taken its toll on them.

As I previously mentioned, in addition to the toll it took on my family, Zoë's death permanently altered my relationships with friends, and people in general. I found myself less emotionally available, and more self-isolated. Sometimes I felt easily aggravated by my friends, even though they hadn't changed. This was just another part of the process for me. I believe it was just due to the amount of energy it required to be available for others. Grief took its toll and I do not have as much emotional reserve as I once possessed. It requires a lot of energy to be available and open to other people, and life requires a lot of energy in general most days. But don't shut yourself off to people entirely. If you do, you'll miss out on some really beautiful moments. One of these moments for me came from a lovely woman, named Karen. One day, Karen grabbed my hand and told me about the two sons she had lost. I recognized the weariness of a grieving mother in her eyes. And as she held my hand softly, she told me "It will never get easier, but it *will* get softer." That simple sentiment has stayed with me throughout the years, and it gave me peace that the days would get less heavy. This woman had survived the unimaginable loss of two children, and it gave me some hope that I, too, would survive. Now, those are the words of comfort I offer to other grieving parents.

In addition to the change I felt taking place in my relationships, I was also dealing with the rollercoaster of emotions I was feeling internally. Many of these emotions I had never felt before, and most of them I had never felt this deeply. Two strong emotions I struggled with were anger and control. The day Zoë died, I felt completely out of control. All of these things were happening *to* me, and there was nothing I could do about it. As a coping mechanism, I tried to control everything within my power to control, and I started exhibiting some obsessive compulsions as I tried to regain some sense in my new world. Feeling out of control would lead to anxiety, which would lead to frustration, then anger. I've had to relearn my limits, and learn to ask for help when I need it. I now know that regular, deliberate relaxation, and learning when to not take on as much is important to maintaining my mental health. Therapy has been instrumental in helping me through these emotions.

Many people think of post-traumatic stress (PTS) as something that only happens to people in the military. But this could not be farther from the truth. The death of a child is considered the single worst stressor a person can go through, and it is incredibly traumatic. Since Zoë's murder, I have experienced a multitude of emotional highs and lows. I have created my own coping mechanisms to deal with PTS. Stressors come in all forms and can present themselves differently each day. As a way to maintain control over my situation, and reduce possible PTS triggers, I have become much more guarded. I prefer staying home to being anywhere, and I am incredibly selective in my relationships. I don't take on large, overwhelming projects that I would've been able to do in the past, rather I keep them less demanding. I have to constantly remember to be gentle with myself, as I know this is a lifetime of grief that I will be enduring.

Post-traumatic stress is real. Reliving moments of trauma are frequent. Some days it does not take much to bring the trauma to the forefront, other days I am more resilient. I never know what each day will look like, so it is important to do the work, and to have the proper coping mechanisms in place. I never know what will trigger my PTS. Sometimes it will be small simple words or phrases that will trigger an emotion. Other times it is an off-hand turn-of-phrase like, "Just shoot me." or someone pretending to shoot themselves in the head with their finger pointed like a gun. People generally use this as a phrase to mean that they would rather die than do something they dislike. While I know people do it out of sarcasm, it still triggers me. It brings an image to my mind of Zoë being shot in the head. Then, I must force that image back into its hiding place, and work through a multitude of emotions. These are visions and emotions I cannot quickly erase from my mind. It is important to talk about PTS, and what it looks like for each individual. We hear about it a lot, but we do not always understand what it looks like - triggers, night terrors, reliving moments that you wish you could forget, visualizing moments that you have made up in your head. All these things are associated with post-traumatic stress.

It is not easy. No book can tell you exactly how to do this. Every person grieves and copes in their own way. Reading books by other grieving parents, helped me realize that there is no one "best way" to grieve. No one knows how they will react to a tragic death and being overly critical of yourself is unnecessary.

CHAPTER 13
GUILT, REGRET AND CLOSURE

L ooking back, it is so easy to judge myself and feel guilt over every decision I've made. Oh, the things I would go back and change if I could. As a young mother, I constantly second-guessed myself. Although there are many great parenting books, no amount of books fully prepare you for the reality of parenthood. I learned to be a mother by becoming one. I struggled to maintain the "perfect" façade after Rayden was born. Having him while I was still a child myself made me feel as though I had to compensate for my lack of knowledge and life experience. As I have gotten older it has become easier to let go of the "do everything correctly" part of parenting, and I have eased up on myself over the years. This type of guilt is normal and most parents feel it to some extent over the years.

After losing Zoë, I felt another form of guilt, in regard to the last few months of Zoë's life. In those few months before she died, I was ending one big relationship, starting a new one, and focusing on my own happiness. I was putting myself first, and I got caught up in my personal issues. Getting caught up in divorce and my selfish need to be happy resulted in lost time with my children, and I abandoned their needs during that time. This type of guilt is incredibly hard to deal with because there are no second chances to make things better with her. I cannot fix what was broken. I have been trying to move forward from how I feel, but I think this will be with me for an exceptionally long time. This is one of those guilts that needs time, lots of journaling, and probably many therapy sessions to help overcome.

I think it is natural to hold onto some regret after someone dies, and play the "what if" and "if I had only" games. Let me tell you from experience: There is no winner in these games. I realize now that dwelling on my past mistakes does little more than make me wish for something that I will never have. I only know that I can hope for forgiveness and do better moving forward. For me, moving forward required humility to acknowledge my mistakes, and strength to own up to my actions.

It has been important for me to take responsibility for my myself and be mindful in the way I care for others moving forward. Years after the fact, I found myself feeling guilt and regret over how I handled things in the first few weeks after

Zoë's death. I've had to make peace with my actions as I processed this part of my grief. Torturing myself with the hurt I may, or may not, have caused will only keep me trapped, and won't allow me to heal and move forward. Working toward forgiving myself has only benefitted my growth.

We cannot go back, we cannot turn back time, for if we could our loved ones would still be here. The only thing we can change is our perspective of what we did to survive during the worst traumas of our lives. When I find myself struggling with guilt, regret, closure, or any other "hitch" on my journey to healing, I find that it helps me to journal, get outside to take in some fresh air, talk to my therapist, or reach out to other bereaved parents that understand what I am going through.

"Closure means finality; a letting go of what once was. Finding Closure implies a complete acceptance of what has happened and honoring of the transition away from what is finished to something new." – google definition

Throughout this book, I've mentioned certain things that have offered me bits of closure after Zoë's death. Closure has been defined as complete acceptance or a letting go of what has happened, with finality. By that definition, closure does not sound like anything I want at all. I do not want to accept Zoë's murder, nor will I ever have complete acceptance of it. But I've also heard of closure described as transitioning away from what is finished to something new. While I will never be finished with her memory, I honor her and carry her memory with me into each new chapter of my life. I think it is common to worry that closure is like betrayal. Many of us get stuck here and we feel guilt for moving forward. But closure is important so that we can move forward and walk over the bridge to healing.

CHAPTER 14
HEALING THRU WELLNESS

Initially, I created my website, Healing Thru Wellness, as a place to journal my thoughts, and share my journey with others. I wanted a place to shed light on my journey, share what healing looked like through my eyes, and be a resource for anyone struggling. My site not only serves to tell my tragic story, but it is a place for healing, for hope, and for positive resources to help others walk though their grief journey.

Creating my page was scary at first, but I was emboldened when I thought of how many people it would help. I've received so many beautiful messages, thanking me for sharing my story. I'm so grateful that I've been able to shed some light on the different feelings that accompany grief, and serve as a beacon of someone who has been through it and survived. My readers fuel my desire to do and say more, and to share my journey, as painful as it may be.

Creating this online community has brought so many other bereaved parents into my life, and I'm blessed to be able to share and learn from their experiences. Receiving guidance from those that have been carrying the weight for a long time has helped me feel less lonely in the world. In turn, providing hope to others has played a big role in bringing me back to wellness. It has helped me find the drive to be healthy and thriving instead of withering away, consumed by depression.

As my mind began to heal, I started hearing cues from my body that it, too, was ready to heal. My body started to crave proper nutrition, and those workouts that it missed so much from before the tragedy. Healing my body has begun to reset the hormonal imbalance that occurred when I let myself shut-down. Re-balancing mind and body has made huge changes in my overall health. I know it will take some time to fully heal my body and get back to the level of health I once maintained, but I am also okay if it's not perfect. I am a different person now, life has changed, and I have changed, and I will continue to be kind and gentle when it comes to my health and wellbeing.

My Healing Thru Wellness website has grown into a wonderful place to share other aspects of my life, including my struggle with infertility. I felt it was important to acknowledge these struggles on my site because I know that losses come in all different forms. We are all struggling in one way or another. No loss is greater than any other loss and everyone's losses are significant. When I look at other people's lives and the struggles that they have chosen to share, it shows me that I am not alone, and that I can, and will survive. Other survivors have been a great source of strength in my life, providing the encouragement to keep moving forward.

Another thing that I share on Healing Thru Wellness is how my hobbies have really helped me during stressful or emotional times. I taught myself to crochet soon after Zoë passed, and I found that it gave my hands something to do when my mind was racing. The rhythmic movement of the crochet hook calms my mind and brings focus. I've turned my emotional energy into many things, including one hundred newborn hats that I donated to the hospital where I was born. This also helped to heal my heart after my miscarriages. Hobbies have been a great distraction, and I have finished many crochet projects, canned preserves, sourdough bread loaves, and now my first book.

As I make strides in my overall wellness, my grief becomes a little less heavy. Choosing a healthier lifestyle will strengthen my body to carry the heavier burden. It's just like getting stronger in the gym – the weight becomes easier to bear as I get stronger. We must remember, there is no timeline in grieving. Grief is something I will carry with me for my lifetime.

There is no set end date as to when I must be done with grief or when I need to move forward with my life. The important thing is that I keep moving forward.

ACKNOWLEDGMENTS

For many years I have struggled with how to honor Zoë. Since losing her, I desire to forever honor her life, to remind people that she lived, and to leave her with a legacy of love. I have since created the Zoë Raine Galasso Memorial Scholarship that will be awarded annually to a Marysville-Pilchuck High School graduating senior. A portion of the sale of this book will go into this fund to symbolize the gift of education that I was unable to provide for my daughter.

I have always been so thankful for the outpouring of support I receive from people all over the world, and I will never be able to thank everyone enough. Many people have told me I should write my story, but I hesitated because I did not want to be perceived as someone who does anything for personal gain. I am a helper, compassionate, and willing to give the shirt off my back to anyone in need. This is when I realized that this was not personal gain, this *was* helping. Telling my story is how I could help other grieving parents feel less alone. Even if only one sentence in the entire book resonates with one person and makes their grief just that much easier to bear, this will all be worth it.

And so, I write. I write to help others heal, I write to honor my daughter and leave her my legacy of love. I write to help myself heal, and to provide strength to anyone who may be in need. I write in the hope that my story will help someone get off that floor, when their world has crumbled into a million pieces. I write to tell you that you are going to survive this.

I cannot put into words how appreciative I am of how I got to this place. The grief has never left, but Karen was right, it has become softer. It has taken me six years to get to this place where I can openly talk about my loss. My tears still fall, because I have accepted my new normal and I have come to terms with the loss of my daughter. But I can now put my focus on honoring her memory.

Blessed is an understatement when I think about my family, more friends, and acquaintances than I can count, and close friends that have become family. Because of your continued love and support, I have been able to get to where I am today.

To my husband Simon, who has been through a whirlwind of highs and lows with me. If we can make it through all that we have been through, we can survive anything life has in store for us. Thank you for being a devoted husband and father, and for your patience and calm demeanor to balance out my crazy. Your belief in my dreams, is all I needed to make this book a reality.

Rayden, my first born, you bring me joy with everything you do, I am so proud to be your mom. I cannot wait to see what the future has in store for you.

Lotte, I hope the memories we share with you of Zoë will bring you joy, knowing that you will always have a big sister in your heart.

Mom, there is no love like your love and devotion to your children and grandbabies, we are so blessed to call you mom and Grammy.

Dad, you are the pillar of our family, strong when we need you and soft around the edges. You are full of emotions that show your family how much we are loved.

Scott, Megan, Jaxon, and Eli, thank you for being the best brother, sister in law and nephews. As the older sister, I delight in the fact that I got to take care of my little brother. I found a new level of respect for you when it was I that needed the care and you and Megan were more than willing and able to step in.

We have been through a nightmare, ALL of us. Losing Zoë took a lot from us all and changed our family dynamic. I am thankful for all the love and support we have been able to wrap around each other over the years.

To Zoë's dad, Mike. Your love for your children has always shown true, they could not have asked for a more loving and caring father.

To my in-laws Charlotte, Jim, and Jacob, thank you for your unconditional love and support, meeting me for the first time amidst tragedy, and opening your hearts and taking me in, always caring and always available.

To Vicki, for jumping on that airplane to be by my side, care for me, and get me through that first week. True friendship knows no boundaries.

Keegan, thank you for always calling to check in, for allowing me to be godparent to your beautiful son, Parker, and for all the positive energy that you provide.

Mariah, thank you for always stepping in and taking control, making all the tough decisions, creating beautiful keepsakes in honor of Zoë, and knowing what I needed without asking.

Lindsey, I appreciated all the laughs and wine nights. Thank you for cleaning my house and holding my hand through all the rough times.

To Julie who rushed to be with me at the hospital that day, we had not seen each other in years, but I will never forget that you came.

To Diana who held me up and kept me going each day. I will never forget our walks, casino trips and adventures of healing we went on together.

To Zoë's best friend, Paige thank you for treating me as your second mamma, and for always checking in on me. I love you and your family.

To my friend, Jacqie, who has spent countless hours listening to me vent about life. You validate me when I need it and have been the best shoulder to cry on. Thank you for believing in me, and always being there.

Robert and Bridie for coming from across the island to help. For writing Zoë's obituary for me and sitting with the family.

My medium, Terri Strauss, who has become a dear friend, thank you for the peace that was given to me, and the closure that I needed. Thank you for giving me the vision two years ago, to write my story. www.terristrauss.com

My friend, Dr. Jeannine Bennett, who knew what to say to get me to jump-start this project. Her knowledge as a life coach and mentor allowed me to feel comfortable taking this step forward. Jeannine is the CEO of Vision to Purpose, www.visiontopurpose.com , and the author of *Broken to Beautiful*.

Alex for your continued empathy and compassion towards my family, and during your reporting of this tragedy.

My therapist Angela, for validating me and allowing me a safe place to heal and communicate my feelings.

I would also like to thank the courageous first responders who responded that day, confronting the tragic scene on October 24th, 2014. The City of Marysville, City of Everett, Providence

Hospital, Washington State Crime Victims Program, Naval Base Everett, Remedy Athletics (formerly CrossFit Marysville), Dr. Boekenoogen, DDS, Shaefer Shipman Funeral home, Word of life Lutheran Brethren church.

Thank you to everyone that donated to the GoFundMe account set up by my friend, Corey. When tragedy strikes, having the financial burden alleviated makes everything easier to grasp as you are already drowning, and for that, I cannot thank everyone enough.

To all the students at school that day and to anyone that was directly impacted by this tragedy, I send you peace, surround you with love, and offer you hope as you continue your path to healing.

RECOMMENDATIONS

Ways to Improve Wellness

- Increase your water intake
- Join a gym, or hire a trainer for motivation
- Find a life or grief coach
- Make healthier food choices
- Work with a dietician to help you get started
- Learn a new hobby
- Schedule coffee dates with a friend
- Make time to connect with your spouse again
- Find a group to participate in, i.e.: book club, walking group, crochet circle, etc.
- Stretch or practice yoga
- Meditate
- Go for long walks
- Make regular time for self-care
- Volunteer or give to charity

Coping Checklist

- Accept your feelings and express them
- Reach out for help
- Consider counseling
- Allow yourself time to mourn

- Treasure and celebrate the life of your loved one
- Try to keep a routine
- Avoid substance abuse to numb the pain
- Be patient with yourself
- Write and reflect in a journal
- Try not to make big decisions in the middle of a crisis
- Let yourself have the relief of a good cry
- Realize it is **okay** to be happy again
- Accept that it is **okay** to not be ok
- Consider grief groups
- Set boundaries for yourself, and the people around you
- Plan ahead
- Know that it is **okay** to say no

Important Phone Numbers

911

National Suicide Prevention Lifeline, 1-800-273-8255

suicidepreventionlifeline.org

National Alliance on Mental Illness, 1-800-950-6264

nami.org

Crisis Response Network, 1-800-203-2273

crisisnetwork.org

RECOMMENDED BOOKS

On Grief and Grieving: Finding the Meaning of Grief Through the Five Stages of Loss by Elisabeth Kübler-Ross, M.D. & David Kessler

Finding Meaning: The Sixth Stage of Grief by David Kessler

Awakening from Grief: Finding the Way Back to Joy by John E. Welshons

Roses in December: Comfort for the Grieving Heart by Marilyn Willet Heavilin

Journey to Healing: A Mother's Guide to Navigating Child Loss by Lisa K. Boehm

When You Think About It: A Fact-finding Journey to Discover My Daughter's Eternal Home, and the Knowledge I Wish I Had While Raising Her by Cynthia M. Mitchell

*"...you are my **rainbow** to keep. My eyes will always be watching you; never will I lose sight of you."*

~ Vesna M. Bailey

"Perhaps the stars in the sky are loved ones letting us know they are nearby guiding us through the night."

-Eskimo Legend

"A wife who loses a husband is called a widow. A husband who loses a wife is called a widower. A child who loses his parents is called an orphan. There is no word for a parent who loses a child. That's how awful the loss is."

-Jay Neugeboren

Remember Me

"Fill not your hearts with pain and sorrow but remember me in every tomorrow. Remember the joy, the laughter, the smiles, I have only gone to rest a little while.

Although my leaving causes pain and grief, my going has eased my hurt, and given me relief. So, dry your eyes and remember me, not as I am now, but as I used to be.

Because I will always remember you all and look on with a smile. Understand in your hearts, I have only gone to rest a little while.

As long as I have the love of each of you, I can live my life in the hearts of all of you."

-Courtesy of Shaefer-Shipman Funeral home

PHOTO PAGES

Zoë's headstone at the Marysville Cemetery, Marysville, Washington.

The heart-shaped rock I found with Rayden on a weekend getaway.

Zoë's rainbow from kindergarten.

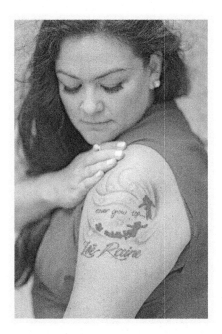

My tattoo of Zoë's "Never Grow Up" drawing. Photo Credit:
Christal Marshall, Virginia Marketing and Media

Zoë and her favorite sweater

The mother-daughter necklaces we shared.

A rainbow behind us in family photos in Virginia Beach,
Virginia. Photo credit: Time to Shine Photography with Tanya

A rainbow outside of my work.

A rainbow from our last hike.

Zoë's art.

Zoë, looking toward her future.

"You are always so Beautiful"

JOURNALING PROMPTS

I found that in my grief journey, journaling has been, and continues to be, a great source of comfort and growth. Journaling has allowed me to release a lot of negative emotions, as there is something about getting them on paper that gives me a new perspective on them. Journaling can be a great catharsis for many people. Below, you'll find a number of journaling prompts to help you process some of the emotions that you're feeling. I encourage you to keep your journal some place that you have no fear of someone finding it. When you know your journal is private, you will be much more likely to be extremely open, honest, and raw. The most healing will come when you are completely vulnerable.

- Write about your favorite memory of your loved one. Describe the sounds, smells, feelings, and mood surrounding your memory. Write down every detail you can remember.

- Write about all the ways that your loss has made you more resilient.

- What calluses have you built up against little things that used to bother you, but now seem unworthy of your time?

- What part of the "old you" do you miss the most?

- Write down every detail you remember about the day your loved one died, both before and after.

- Do a brain dump. Write everything you're thinking and feeling. It feels good to get it all out.

- Write a letter to your deceased loved one. What would you say if you had the chance?

- Write letters to your living loved ones. Say all the things you'd want to say if this was your last chance to say it.

- Write down all of the ugly thoughts in your head. Write down all of the mean things you wish you could say, and all of the hateful thoughts. Get the ugliness out of your heart and onto paper. When you're done, burn the pages and say goodbye to the bitterness and hatred.

- Count your blessings. Write about all the good things in your life from the little things to the big things.

- Write about what you would do if you had one more day with your loved one. Plan the day from the moment you wake up to the moment you go to bed.

- Write a letter to the thing or person responsible for taking your loved one from you. Tell them how you feel, and all of the thoughts you have surrounding their part in the loss of your loved one.

- Write a letter to yourself. Take on the role of someone who cares about you deeply. Write all the nurturing things you need to hear and reread the letter when you're feeling discouraged.

- Write about what you need right now. What do you need to get through one more day? Make sure these are *attainable* things. Then go after what you need!

- What things in your life prepared you for what you're going through right now?

- Write about the range of emotions you've felt since your loss.

- Write about all the ways you can honor your loved one. Is there some sort of memorial you'd like to do for them but haven't? If so, make a list of the steps you need to take to accomplish the memorial.

- Chose a song that reminds you of your loved one. Write the lyrics down.

- How can you love yourself more?

- Write about the guilt you may be feeling about feeling joy again. Why is that guilt unjustified?

- Write about the place that you feel closest to your loved one. Be as detailed as possible.

- Write a future for yourself. Look at where you are now, and where you want to be. Write about the steps you could take to get to where you want to be.

- How do you feel spiritually since your loss? Are you struggling to make sense of things, or have you found peace as a result of your beliefs?

- Do you believe that your loved one sends you signs? If so, write about them.

- Write thank you letters to the people that rallied around you after your loss. You may choose to send the letters or keep them.

- When do you feel the safest?

- How has your loss changed the way you interact in the world?

- Write down all the things you wish you could say to people that treat you differently since your loss.

- What are some of your coping mechanisms? Which ones are beneficial for your overall well-being, and which ones are detrimental?

- Is there guilt or regret that seems to be holding you back from moving forward or from healing?

- What brings you a sense of peace? How can you have more of that peace in your life?

- What are some of your grief triggers?

- How has your health changed since your loss? What

are some steps you could take to take better care of yourself and those who depend on you?

- The seven stages of grief (according to the Kubler-Ross model) are shock, denial, anger, bargaining, depression, testing, and acceptance. What stage(s) do you find yourself in?

- What do you miss the most about your loved one?

- What are you going to do now that your loved one is gone?

- What was the best thing that your loved one taught you about life?

- What are some things you've learned about yourself through this experience?

- What are you willing to do to help yourself heal?

- What memory always makes you smile?

- What are some negative thoughts you would like to reduce?

- What are some positive thoughts you would like to increase?

- What are you having a hard time understanding?

- What are you ready to let go of?

- If the situation were reversed, and *you* were the one who died, what would you say to your loved one that is still alive? What would you say to comfort them? Do you think they would say the same to you?

ABOUT THE AUTHOR

Michelle Jeffreys has worked as a health and wellness coach for fifteen years. Many of those years, she spent working for the U.S. Navy as a Fitness and Nutrition professional. Michelle created Healing thru Wellness as a site dedicated to her blog and this book in honor of her daughter. She is married to Simon, and a mother to three; Rayden, Zoë, and Lotte. She enjoys walking, cooking, boating, fishing, and crochet. Born and raised in Everett, Washington she currently resides with her family in Virginia Beach, Virginia.

About Healing Thru Wellness

Michelle created the website as a place to blog and reach people who deal with grief, disbelief, child loss, tragedy, and that awful feeling of being alone. She wanted a place to journal her thoughts as they came, and to share those thoughts and feelings with others. A place to shed light on her journey, what that looked like through her eyes, and to be a resource for anyone struggling. The site is not only to tell her tragic story, but a place for healing, for hope and to provide some positive resources.

This site is also a memorial to her daughter, the legacy she left behind, and a place to reminisce over photos and memories. You will find some of her daughter's artwork and photos as well as information on the memorial scholarship in her name.

www.healingthruwellness.com

THE ZOË RAINE GALASSO MEMORIAL SCHOLARSHIP

The Zoë Raine Galasso Memorial Scholarship is very dear to my heart. I began working on a scholarship for my daughter soon after she died. It was my way of honoring her while also giving back to the community that held me up during the most difficult time in my life.

For 14 incredible years, Zoë was a gift not just to my family and me, but to those who knew her. Zoë had great thoughts about her future; education was important to her. Offering a scholarship to help others pursue their academic dreams gives me great comfort, and I know it would make Zoë smile.

ANNUAL SCHOLARSHIP DONATION:

The Marysville Rotary Education Foundation was selected due to their mission of helping students achieve their higher education studies.

If you are interested in donating to the Zoë Raine Galasso Memorial Scholarship, please follow the below guidance:

Funds are being accepted by the Marysville Rotary Education Foundation. The address is provided for your convenience.

Address:
Marysville Rotary Education Foundation
c/o Zoë Raine Galasso Memorial Scholarship
P.O. Box 1875
Marysville, Washington 98270

Please make checks out to: **Marysville Rotary Education Foundation**

IMPORTANT: Please make sure to attach a note with your check stating the funds are to be allocated to the Zoë Raine Galasso Memorial Scholarship.

SCHOLARSHIP APPLICATION DETAILS:

The Marysville Rotary Education Foundation is a non-profit 501(c)(3) corporation formed in 1996. As stated in the Foundation's Articles of Incorporation, the general purposes of the Foundation are to ...*provide support and promote general and vocational education and scholarships for the students in the greater Marysville area.*

The Foundation fulfills these purposes by awarding secondary education scholarships and making education project grants in the community.

The Foundation will consider grant applications focusing on such areas as primary or secondary education, adult literacy/numeracy and education, English as a second language and "at risk" or disadvantaged learners.

All donations are significant. The Foundation has developed and endowment fund that will draw interest and dividends. These earnings will then provide the scholarship funding for future generations. Outright gifts, annual donations, and bequests are options for giving. The rotary Education Foundation can provide donors with an advisor to help determine the best way for you to give. All donations can be confidential or public in manner. We welcome our community members to join in and help Rotary build a solid foundation for giving in the future.

To learn more about the Marysville Rotary Education Foundation, their Scholarships and how to apply, please go to www.thewashboard.org. You can also search their site at https://portal.clubrunner.ca/275/sitepage/marysville-rotary-education-foundation.

ONE LAST THING...

A letter to bereaved parents and to those who care about them.

Dear bereaved parent,

I am so sorry that you are here. You have experienced the unimaginable; your pain and sorrow know no bounds. Be gentle with yourself; allow yourself to grieve this tremendous loss. There is no timeline, for there is no loss like that of a child. Children should never leave us before their time.

Healing takes time, and there is no definitive because we will carry this for the rest of our lives. Being understood by those around you who do not know the depth of your grief will take time. You are not alone, reach out to those that have walked this long walk before you.

Let us help carry your pain and guide you when you feel lost. Cry, cry some more, and when you are ready, move forward in honor of your child in a light that makes you proud.

Dear Caregivers of the Bereaved,

Please be gentle and patient with us, for we cannot control our emotions during this time. We may cry, scream, or say hurtful things. Our anger may be at the forefront every day, but we appreciate you. Our hearts are broken, and only time and compassion can mend them. We are having difficulty making decisions and understanding our needs, so we will need you to step in and take care of the things we have forgotten. If we have not said this enough, we are grateful. Thank you!

Sincerely,

A Bereaved Parent

Made in the USA
Monee, IL
24 October 2020